This journal belongs to

Leviticus 19:18 but thou shalt love thy neighbor as thyself: I am Jehovah.

Leviticus 19:18 but thou shalt love thy neighbor as thyself: I am Jehovah.

Deuteronomy 7:8 But it was because the Lord loved you and kept the oath he swore to your ancestors that he brought you out with a mighty hand and redeemed you from the land of slavery, from the power of Pharaoh king of Egypt.

Deuteronomy 7:9 Know therefore that the Lord your God is God; he is the faithful God, keeping his covenant of love to a thousand generations of those who love him and keep his commandments.

Deuteronomy 7:13 He will love you and bless you and increase your numbers. He will bless the fruit of your womb, the crops of your land—your grain, new wine, and olive oil.

Deuteronomy 10:12 what does the Lord your God ask of you but to fear the Lord your God, to walk in obedience to him, to love him, to serve the Lord your God with all your heart and with all your soul.

Deuteronomy 30:16 For I command you today to love the Lord your God, to walk in obedience to him, and to keep his commands, decrees, and laws then you will live and increase, and the Lord your God will bless you in the land you are entering to possess.

Deuteronomy 30:20 love the Lord your God, listen to his voice, and hold fast to him. For
the Lord is your life, and he will give you many years
in the land he swore to give to your fathers

Psalm 5:11 Spread your Protection over them,
that those who love your name may rejoice in you.

Psalm 11:7 For the Lord is righteous, he loves justice the upright will see his face.

Psalm 13:5 But I trust in your unfailing love, my heart rejoices in your salvation.

Psalm 17:7 Show me the wonders of your great love, you who save by your right hand those who take refuge in you from their foes.

Psalm 25:7 Do not remember the sins of my youth and my rebellious ways; according to your love remember me, for you Lord are good.

Psalm 31:16 Let your face shine on your servant
save me in your unfailing love.

Psalm 33:5 The Lord loves righteousness and justice
the earth is full of his unfailing love.

Psalm 33:18 But the eyes of the Lord are on those who fear him,
on those whose hope is in his unfailing love

Psalm 36:5 Your love, Lord, reaches to the heavens, your faithfulness to the skies.

Psalm 36:5 Your love, Lord, reaches to the heavens, your faithfulness to the skies.

Psalm 37:28 For the Lord loves the just and will not forsake his faithful ones.

Psalm 37:28 For the Lord loves the just and will not forsake his faithful ones.

Psalm 59:16 But I will sing of your strength, in the morning I will sing of your love for you are my fortress, my refuge in times of trouble.

*Psalm 69:39 The children of his servants shall inherit it,
and those who love his name will dwell there.*

Psalm 86:13 For great is your love toward me;

you have delivered me from the depths, from the realm of the dead.

Psalm 89:1 I will sing of the Lord's great love forever with my mouth, I will make your faithfulness known through all generations.

*Psalm 91:14 Because he loves me, says the Lord, I rescue him:
I will protect him for he acknowledges my name.*

Psalm 97:10 Let those who love the Lord hate evil, for he guards the lives of his faithful ones and delivers them from the hand of the wicked.

Psalm 103:8 The Lord is compassionate and gracious, slow to anger, abounding in love.

Psalm 103:8 The Lord is compassionate and gracious, slow to anger, abounding in love.

Psalm 107:1 Give thanks to the Lord, for he is good,
his love endures forever.

Psalm 108:4 For great is your love, higher than the heavens;
your faithfulness reaches to the skies.

Psalm 119:97 Oh how I love your law! I meditate on it all day long.

Psalm 119:127 Therefore I love your commandments above gold, even fine gold.

Proverbs 3:3 Let love and faithfulness never leave you, bind them around your neck, write them on the tablet of your heart.

Proverbs 4:6 Do not forsake wisdom, and she will protect you, love her and she will watch over you.

Proverbs 8:17 I love those who love me, and those who seek me find me.

Proverbs 8:17 I love those who love me, and those who seek me find me.

Proverbs 18:21 The tongue has the power of life and death,
and those who love it will eat its fruit.

Proverbs 19:8 The one who gets wisdom loves life. The one who cherishes understanding will soon prosper.

Proverbs 20:28 Love and faithfulness keep a king safe

through love, his throne is made secure.

Proverbs 22:11 One who loves a pure heart and who speaks with grace will have the king for a friend.

Proverbs 27:5 Better is open rebuke than love that is hidden.

Proverbs 27:5 Better is open rebuke than love that is hidden.

Proverbs 29:3 A man who loves wisdom brings joy to his father,
but a companion of prostitutes squanders his wealth.

Song of Solomon 2:4 Let him lead me to the banquet hall,
and let his banner over me be love.

Isaiah 38:17 In your love you kept me from the pit of destruction;
you have put all my sins behind your back.

Isaiah 61:8 For I, the Lord, love justice, I hate robbery and wrong doing. In my faithfulness, I will reward my people and make an everlasting covenant with them.

Isaiah 63:9 In his love and mercy he redeemed them;
he lifted them; up and carried them all the days of old.

Jeremiah 31:3 The Lord appeared to us in the past, saying: "I have loved you with an everlasting love." I have drawn you with unfailing kindness.

Jeremiah 33:11 "Give thanks to the Lord Almighty, for the Lord is good, his love endures forever." For I will restore the fortunes of the land as they were before, says the Lord.

Daniel 9:4 I prayed to the Lord my God and confessed: "Lord, the great and awesome God, who keeps his covenant of love with those who love him and keep his commandments

Hosea 2:23 I will plant her for myself in the land;
I will show my love to the one I called 'Not my loved one.'
I will say to those called 'Not my people,' 'You are my people';
and they will say, 'You are my God.'"

Hosea 12:6 But you must return to your God;
maintain love and justice, and wait for your God always.

Amos 5:15 Hate evil, love good
maintain justice in the courts.
Perhaps the Lord God Almighty
will have mercy on the remnant of Joseph.

Jonah 4:2 I knew that you are a gracious and compassionate God, slow to anger and abounding in love, a God who relents from sending calamity.

Micah 6:8 And what does the Lord require of you?
To act justly and to love mercy and to walk humbly with your God.

Zephaniah 3:17 The Lord your God is with you,
the Mighty Warrior who saves. He will take great delight in you;
in his love, he will no longer rebuke you, but will rejoice over you with singing."

Matthew 3:17 And a voice from heaven said,
"This is my Son, whom I love with him, I am well pleased.

Matthew 5:43 "You have heard that it was said, "
Love your neighbor and hate your enemy."

Matthew 5:44 But I tell you, love your enemies and pray for those who persecute you

Matthew 6:24 "No one can serve two masters. Either you will hate the one and love the other, or you will be devoted to the one and despise the other. You cannot serve both God and money.

Matthew 19:19 honor your father and mother, and love your neighbor as yourself.

Matthew 19:19 honor your father and mother, and love your neighbor as yourself.

Mark 1:11 And a voice came from heaven:
"You are my Son, whom I love with you, I am well pleased."

Mark 12:30 Love the Lord your God with all your heart and with all your soul and with all your mind and with all your strength.

Luke 6:35 But love your enemies, do good to them, and lend to them without expecting to get anything back. Then your reward will be great, and you will be children of the Most High because he is kind to the ungrateful and wicked.

Luke 10:27 He answered, `Love the Lord your God with all your heart and with all your soul and with all your strength and with all your mind'
and, `Love your neighbor as yourself.'

John 5:20 For the Father loves the Son and shows him all he does. Yes, and he will show him even greater works than these, so that you will be amazed.

John 13:35 By this everyone will know that you are my disciples if you love one another.

John 14:21 Whoever has my commands and keeps them is the one who loves me. The one who loves me will be loved by my Father, and I too will love them and show myself to them.

John 14:23 Jesus replied, "Anyone who loves me will obey my teaching. My Father will love them, and we will come to them and make our home with them.

John 14:28 "You heard me say, 'I am going away and I am coming back to you.' If you loved me, you would be glad that I am going to the Father, for the Father is greater than I.

John 14:31 but he comes so that the world may learn that I love the Father and do exactly what my Father has commanded me.

John 15:12 My command is this: Love each other as I have loved you.

John 16:27 No, the Father himself loves you because you have loved me
and have believed that I came from God.

John 17:26 I have made you known to them, and will continue to make you known in order that the love you have for me may be in them and that I myself may be in them.

John 21:15 When they had finished eating, Jesus said to Simon Peter,
"Simon son of John, do you love me more than these?"
"Yes, Lord," he said, "you know that I love you." Jesus said, "Feed my lambs."

John 21:16 Again Jesus said, "Simon son of John, do you love me?"
He answered, "Yes, Lord, you know that I love you." Jesus said,
"Take care of my sheep."

Romans 5:5 And hope does not put us to shame, because God's love has been poured out into our hearts through the Holy Spirit, who has been given to us.

Romans 5:8 But God demonstrates his own love for us in this:
While we were still sinners, Christ died for us.

Roman 8:28 And we know that in all things God works for the good of those who love him, who have been called according to his purpose.

Romans 8:35 Who shall separate us from the love of Christ? Shall trouble or hardship or persecution or famine or nakedness or danger or sword? Romans 8:37 No, in all these things we are more than conquerors through him who loved us.

Romans 8:39 neither height nor depth, nor anything else in all creation, will be able to separate us from the love of God that is in Christ Jesus our Lord.

Romans 13:8 [Love Fulfills the Law] Let no debt remain outstanding, except the continuing debt to love one another, for whoever loves others has fulfilled the law.

Romans 13:9 Love your neighbor as yourself.

Romans 15:30 I urge you, brothers and sisters, by our Lord Jesus Christ and by the love of the Spirit, to join me in my struggle by praying to God for me.

1 Corinthians 2:9 "What no eye has seen, what no ear has heard, and what no human mind has conceived" — the things God has prepared for those who love him—

1 Corinthians 4:21 What do you prefer? Shall I come to you with a rod of discipline, or shall I come in love and with a gentle spirit?

*1 Corinthians 8:1 [Concerning Food Sacrificed to Idols] Now about food sacrificed to idols: We know that "We all possess knowledge."
But knowledge puffs up while love builds up.*

1 Corinthians 13:3 If I give all I possess to the poor and give over my body to hardship that I may boast, but do not have love, I gain nothing.

1 Corinthians 13:4 Love is patient, love is kind. It does not envy, it does not boast, it is not proud.

1 Corinthians 13:13 And now these three remain: faith, hope, and love.
But the greatest of these is love.

1 Corinthians 16:24 My love to all of you in Christ Jesus. Amen.

1 Corinthians 16:24 My love to all of you in Christ Jesus. Amen.

2 Corinthians 8:24 Therefore show these men the proof of your love and the reason for our pride in you, so that the churches can see it.

2 Corinthians 13:11 Finally, brothers and sisters, rejoice! Strive for full restoration, encourage one another, be of one mind, live in peace. And the God of love and peace will be with you.

2 Corinthians 13:14 May the grace of the Lord Jesus Christ, and the love of God, and the fellowship of the Holy Spirit be with you all.

Galatians 2:20 The life I now live in the body, I live by faith in the Son of God, who loved me and gave himself for me.

Galatians 5:6 The only thing that counts is faith expressing itself through love.

Galatians 5:13 [Life by the Spirit] You, my brothers and sisters, were called to be free. But do not use your freedom to indulge the flesh

rather, serve one another humbly in love.

Galatians 5:22-23 But the fruit of the Spirit is love, joy, peace, forbearance, kindness, goodness, faithfulness

gentleness and self-control.

Ephesians 1:4 For he chose us in him before the creation of the world to be holy and blameless in his sight. In love.

Ephesians 4:2 Be completely humble and gentle; be patient, bearing with one another in love.

Ephesians 4:2 Be completely humble and gentle; be patient, bearing with one another in love.

Ephesians 4:15 Speaking truth in love, we will grow to become in every respect the mature body of him who is the head, that is, Christ.

Ephesians 4:16 From him the whole body, joined and held together by every supporting ligament, grows and builds itself up in love, as each part does its work.

Ephesians 5:1 Follow God's Example, therefore, as dearly loved children

Ephesians 5:28 In this same way, husbands ought to love their wives as their own bodies. He who loves his wife loves himself.

Ephesians 5:33 However, each one of you also must love his wife as he loves himself, and the wife must respect her husband.

Ephesians 6:24 Grace to all who love our Lord Jesus Christ with an undying love.

Philippians 1:9 And this is my prayer: that you love may abound yet more and more in knowledge depth of insight

Philippians 4:8 Finally, brothers and sisters, whatever is true, whatever is noble, whatever is right, whatever is pure, whatever is lovely, whatever is admirable–if anything is excellent or praiseworthy–think about such things.

Colossians 1:5 the faith and love that springs from the hope stored up for you in heaven and about which you have already heard in the true message of the gospel

Colossians 1:5 the faith and love that springs from the hope stored up for you in heaven and about which you have already heard in the true message of the gospel

Colossians 2:2 My goal is that they may be encouraged in heart and united in love, so that they may have the full riches of complete understanding, in order that they may know the mystery of God, namely, Christ.

Colossians 3:12 Therefore, as God's chosen people, holy and dearly loved, clothe yourselves with compassion, kindness, humility, gentleness and patience.

1 Thessalonians 1:4 For we know, brothers and sisters loved by God, that he has chosen you,

1 Thessalonians 3:12 May the Lord make your love increase and overflow for each other and everyone else, just as ours does for you

1 Thessalonians 4:9 Now about your love for one another we do not need to write to you,
for you yourselves have been taught by God to love each other.

1 Thessalonians 5:8 But since we belong to the day, let us be sober, putting on faith and love as a breastplate, and the hope of salvation as a helmet.

1 Thessalonians 5:13 Hold them in the highest regard in love because of their work. Live in peace with each other.

Titus 2:2 Teach the older men to be temperate, worthy of respect, self-controlled, and sound in faith, in love and in endurance.

Titus 3:4 But when the kindness and love of God our Savior appeared.

Titus 3:15 Everyone with me sends you greetings. Greet those who love us in the faith. Grace be with you all.

Hebrews 6:10 God is not unjust, he will not forget your work and the love you have shown him as. You have helped his people and continue to help them.

Hebrews 10:24 and let us consider how we may spur one another on toward love and good deeds

Hebrews 13:1 Keep on loving one another as brothers and sisters.

Hebrew 13:5 Keep your lives free from the love of money and be content with what you have because God has said, "Never will I leave you never will I forsake you."

James 1:12 Blessed is the one who perseveres under trial because, having stood the test, that person will receive the crown of life that the Lord has promised to those who love him.

1 Peter 1:22 Now that you have purified yourselves by obeying the truth so that you have sincere love for each other, love one another deeply from the heart.

1 Peter 4:8 Above all, love each other deeply because love covers over a multitude of sins.

1 Peter 4:8 Above all, love each other deeply because love covers over a multitude of sins.

1 Peter 5:14 Greet one another with a kiss of love.
Peace be with you all that are in Christ Jesus.

1 John 2:15 Do not love the world or anything in the world. If anyone loves the world, the love for the Father is not in them.

1 John 2:15 Do not love the world or anything in the world. If anyone loves the world, the love for the Father is not in them.

1 John 3:1 See what great love the Father has lavished on us, that we should be called children of God! And that is what we are!

1 John 3:16 This is how we know what love is: Jesus Christ laid down his life for us. And we ought to lay down our lives for our brothers and sisters

1 John 3:16 This is how we know what love is: Jesus Christ laid down his life for us. And we ought to lay down our lives for our brothers and sisters

1 John 3:18 Dear Children, let us not love with words or
speech but with actions and in truth.

1 John 4:7 [God' Love and Ours] Dear friends, let us love one another, for love comes from God. Everyone who loves has been born of God and knows God.

1 John 4:8 Anyone who does not love does not know God, because God is love.

1 John 4:8 Anyone who does not love does not know God, because God is love.

I John 4:11 Dear friends, since God so loved us, we also ought to love one another.

1 John 4:12 No one has ever seen God, but if we love one another, God lives in us and his love is made complete in us.

1 John 4:18 There is no fear in love. But perfect love drives out fear because fear has to do with punishment. The one who fears is not made perfect in love.

1 John 4:19 We love Him because he first loved us.

1 John 4:19 We love Him because he first loved us.

1 John 4:20 Whoever claims to love God yet hates a brother or sister is a liar. For whoever does not love their brother and sister, whom they have seen, cannot love God, whom they have not seen.

Jude 1:2 Mercy, peace, and love be yours in abundance.

Revelation 2:19 I know your deeds, your love and faith, your service and perseverance, and that you are now doing more than you did at first.

Revelation 2:19 I know your deeds, your love and faith, your service and perseverance, and that you are now doing more than you did at first.

Revelation 3:19 Those whom I love, I rebuke and discipline. So be earnest and repent.